THE SCHOOL OF LOVE:

The Cure For Selfhatred, Guides & Most Effective Way To Learn To Love Oneself.

By

DR NICKI PAIGE

Table Of Content

Introduction

Many mental illnesses have a component at their core that we are not accustomed to seeing on its own as a cause of our misery and self-loathing. Although we can appear to be only concerned about the future, unwilling to get past regrets, or uneasy with other people, the truth is that we might be experts at hating ourselves. It is important to understand and research self-loathing and hatred as one of the biggest sources of suffering and despair. Suicides and loneliness.

One of the reasons self hatred can be so difficult to overcome is the idea that self love is the antidote and treatment for it.

Self-acceptance is the key to overcoming self-hatred and self-loathing, not intensifying self-love. It's not necessary for us to get rid of all of our negative self-talk. While working on self-acceptance, there are various ways in which we can continue to harbor regret and suspicion toward ourselves.

Chapter 1

What Is Self-Loathing or Self-hatred?

Self-hatred is an inclination that looks like self-loathing, as it continually pushes that you're not sufficient. As a result, you could feel as you don't merit love or that terrible things happen to you on purpose.

Self-hatred, or self-loathing, is outrageous analysis of oneself. It might feel like nothing you do is sufficient or that you are contemptible or undeserving of beneficial things throughout everyday life. Self-loathing can embrace a new lease on life chasing after you, the entire day consistently, scrutinizing you and bringing up each defect, or disgracing you for each error.

Self-hatred shows itself through predictable negative contemplations which are intently attached to unnecessary self-analysis. While self-analysis is a solid part of life, it can begin to eclipse other idea designs while you're going through a self-hatred stage.

If self-hatred happens for a really long time, it can prompt more extreme circumstances, similar to wretchedness or substance misuse. Essentially, less significantly, it can prompt viciousness toward others or sensations of inadequacy.

What Is Self-Loathing Behavior?

There are many examples that could be named self-hatred conduct — however they all beginning from over the top self-analysis. Recognizing these is essential for improving, as it will permit you to shut down these idea designs in time the following opportunity they come up.

Normal self-hatred thought designs incorporate inclination that you're a disappointment, that you can't do things right, or that you're not sufficient. Additionally, you could apply a similar disposition to your prosperity, imagining that you're never going to improve.

Self-hatred contemplations can likewise come in regards to explicit circumstances, such as gorging or remaining up past the point of no return. They might try and show up after friendly cooperations, such as retribution that you were excessively forceful or bashful. Other normal repeating self-hatred ways of behaving incorporate holding resentment against yourself for a previous mishap and setting unreasonable assumptions.

Frequently, these examples are connected with out of line correlations we make among ourselves and others. Because of self-hatred, you could wind up feeling mediocre compared to others by disregarding their errors and just perceiving their ideals.

Self-hatred Symptoms

It's difficult to pinpoint the specific side effects of self-hatred, as it's anything but an ailment all alone. However, there are a couple of general signs that an individual may be feeling self-hatred and self-loathing:

Melancholy

Social tension

Self-perception issues

Sensations of uselessness

There are a couple of different signs too — however these don't necessarily highlight self-hatred. Rather, they are more connected with an overabundance of self-analysis, which can ultimately prompt self-loathing.

1 Feelings of culpability at whatever point something turns out badly

2 Perfectionism

3 Self-hurt

4 Eating issues

Commonplace self-loathing contemplations might include:

"I realized I would fizzle.

""For what reason do I by any chance attempt?

"I'm a failure.""

Nobody needs to associate with me.

""Once more, see me messing up.

""Mightn't I at any point be ordinary?

""I can't stand myself."

Chapter 2

What Causes Self-hatred?

Self-hatred ordinarily comes from an earlier time, as most self-detesting propensities create during youth. In particular, they're established in the relationship you had with your folks or guardians.

Since these are the earliest bonds we foster in our lives, they can extraordinarily affect how we see and act in ongoing connections. This normally incorporates our relationship with ourselves — implying that dictator or oppressive parental figures can prompt self-hatred.

Specialists contend that guardians who energize independence and permit their youngsters to commit errors will prompt more self-assurance. In actuality, a parent that is excessively controlling will make an absence of confidence that can ultimately develop into self-hatred. Especially, that's what research recommends, as kids, we relate to the irate guardian rather than with ourselves. This prompts youngsters taking on outrage, dread, and other pessimistic feelings that the parent is going through in snapshots of stress. Thus, we are exposed to circumstances that cause us to feel awful and insufficient.

Finally, it's vital to consider that youngsters can likewise gain self-hatred designs from their guardians — regardless of whether they're not associated with the circumstance. This makes a youngster exceptionally inclined to self-hatred in the event that they notice their folks going through self-despising stages.

What Causes Self-Hate?

Self-loathing creates over the long run. It's normally set off by more than one component, including past injury, compulsiveness, bogus assumptions, social correlations, and a few learned ways of behaving.

It's memorable's vital that not every person who encounters self-loathing will have had a similar educational encounters. There is no solitary way that prompts thinking, "I disdain myself." Consider your special conditions and what could have carried you to this point.

The following are the causes

Negative Inner Critic

Assuming that you are thinking "I disdain myself," odds are you have a negative inward pundit who continually puts you down.1 This basic voice could contrast you with others or let you know that you are not sufficient.

You could feel like you are not quite the same as others and that you don't have the goods. These contemplations might leave you feeling like an outsider or a misrepresentation when you are with others.

The internal pundit is like a pseudo-nemesis who is resolved to subverting your prosperity. This voice in your mind is loaded up with self-loathing, and can likewise advance into neurosis and dubiousness assuming you listen adequately long. The inward pundit doesn't maintain that you should encounter achievement, so it will try and chop you down when you really do achieve something great.

Coming up next are a few things your internal pundit could say:

"Who do you assume you are to do that?

""You are never going to succeed regardless of how enthusiastically you attempt.

""You will wreck this very much like you mess up all the other things.

""How could an individual like that like you? There should be a ulterior thought process.

""You can't confide in anybody. They are about to let you down.

""You should eat that pastry. In any case, you're about to wind up eating an excessive amount of."

In the event that you have a voice in your mind like this, you could come to accept that these kinds of decisive considerations are reality. Assuming the voice lets you know that you are useless, idiotic, or ugly, you could ultimately come to trust those things. Also, with those considerations, comes the conviction that you're not deserving of affection, achievement, certainty, or the opportunity to commit errors.

The more you pay attention to that basic inward voice, the more power you provide for it. Likewise, you could ultimately begin to extend your own uncertainties onto others, leaving you neurotic, dubious, and unfit to acknowledge love and generosity. On the off chance that this sounds like you, odds are you have been paying attention to your negative inward pundit for a really long time.

Where does that negative internal pundit come from? It isn't reasonable that you fostered that voice in your mind without help from anyone else. Rather, most frequently, the negative internal pundit emerges from past bad valuable encounters. These could be youth encounters with your parents,2 tormenting from companions, or even the result of a terrible relationship.

Adolescence Experiences

Did you grow up with guardians who were incredulous of you? Or on the other hand did you have a parent who appeared to be worried, irate, or tense, and who caused you to feel like you expected to tread lightly?

Provided that this is true, you might have figured out how to be peaceful and blur away from plain sight. Youth encounters or injury like maltreatment, disregard, being over-controlled, or being scrutinized can all prompt the improvement of a negative internal voice.

Awful Relationships

Not all basic inward voices start during adolescence. On the off chance that you were seeing someone fellowship with somebody who participated in similar kinds of ways of behaving, the experience could likewise have made a negative internal voice.

This really might incorporate a work relationship with a collaborator or boss with an inclination to put you down or cause you to feel mediocre. Any kind of relationship can possibly establish a negative vibe to you and make a negative internal voice that is difficult to shake.

Tormenting

Is it safe to say that you were the casualty of harassing in school, at work, or in another relationship? Indeed, even transient associations with individuals can make enduring recollections that influence your self-idea and influence your confidence.

Assuming that you end up having flashback recollections of apparently unimportant occasions with menaces from quite a while ago or present, it may be the case that the experience meaningfully affects your brain. Assuming that your negative inward voice replays the expressions of your genuine harassers, you have a more profound work to do to deliver those contemplations instead of incorporate them.

Horrible Mishaps

Have you encountered any horrendous life altering situations like an auto crash, actual assault, or critical misfortune? Assuming this is the case, the misfortune could leave you pondering, "why me?" which can advance into sensations of disgrace or lament, especially on the off chance that you believe you were some way or another to blame.

Ecological Triggers

Long after unique occasions, you could wind up being set off by things that occur in your regular routine. For instance, another collaborator could help you to remember a previous terrible involvement with work, or another companion could set off an upsetting memory from your experience growing up.

Assuming you wind up having a close to home response to a circumstance that appears to be messed up with regards to what has occurred, you might have to accomplish more work to reveal the things that are keeping you down. Many find this cycle is made more straightforward with the assistance of a specialist or other emotional wellness proficient.

Negative Self-Concept

Do you have a negative self-idea, unfortunate mental self portrait, or low confidence? At the point when you have considerations of self-loathing, little issues can be amplified into a lot bigger ones. You might feel like the terrible things that happen are your very own impression inborn "disagreeableness."

For instance, you're at a party and you make a wisecrack that crashes and burns. Rather than adapting to all challenges and continuing on, your negative self-idea could prompt a twisting into negative contemplations, for example, "everybody can't stand me" and "I'll always be unable to make any companions."

Psychological well-being Conditions

An identity disdain could likewise be the consequence of an emotional well-being condition like misery or uneasiness. Sadness, for instance, can cause side effects like sadness, culpability, and disgrace, which can cause you to feel like you are bad enough.4 Unfortunately, the idea of wretchedness additionally implies that you can't see through this mental predisposition to perceive that your downturn is making you maintain this viewpoint.

The more that your condition impacts your considerations, the more probable it is that you will begin to consider this negative perspective on yourself to be your existence. This can leave you feeling like you are not commendable and don't have a place. You might feel detached and not quite the same as every other person.

Injury

Many individuals with outrageous self-loathing have experienced horrible and sincerely testing encounters from before. These encounters frequently incorporate sexual, physical, or psychological mistreatment and disregard.

At the point when youngsters experience injury, they start to see the world as hazardous and individuals around them as perilous. With an end goal to figure out their reality, they might foster a story that causes them to feel as though they are not worth cherishing and have no worth. These contemptuous assertions might have been expressed straightforwardly to them by a parent or other cherished one, and they before long become a very much natural piece of their inward pundit.

Results and conquences of Self-Hatred

Past the reasons for self-loathing, it's essential to comprehend the results that can result when your considerations persistently build up that self-loathing. The following are a few expected results:

You could quit attempting to do things since you feel they will just end badly.You could participate in pointless way of behaving like utilizing substances, eating excessively, or detaching yourself.You could disrupt your own endeavors or neglect to deal with yourself.You could unwittingly pick individuals who are terrible for you or who will exploit you, for example, harmful companions or partners.You might battle with low fearlessness and low self-esteem.You could experience difficulty simply deciding and feel like you really want others to direct you when you become deadened in indecision.You could have a fussbudget propensity and battle to get things done.You could exorbitantly stress over day to day issues or your future.You find it hard to accept beneficial things about yourself and feel like others are being great or manipulative when they praise you.You probably won't have the option to pursue your objectives and dreams and feel held back.You might question your capacities and what you can accomplish.You could see the future as being exceptionally dreary and have no good expectations.You might feel like you don't have a place anyplace and that you are an outsider and separated from your general surroundings.

A large number of the results of self-loathing are like the indications of self-loathing. Along these lines, it turns into an inevitable outcome from which you can only with significant effort escape. However long you stay in this pattern of self-loathing, you won't ever push ahead. Be that as it may, with assistance, you can break the cycle.

Chapter 3

How would I quit detesting myself?

This is a truly hard spot to be, I've been there, crying in the change room at a shop since I don't seem to be the banner in the change room. I can't let you know what compelled me at last emerge from it cause I don't sincerely have the foggiest idea. What's more, I'm flawed now, still somewhat broken yet not at the profundities of that self-hatred. In any case, I can perceive you a few things that made a difference.

begin moving. I don't be guaranteed to mean you want to begin siphoning iron however basically take a walk every day, get outside and move. It might just be 20mins, yet the sun and moving will do you great, particularly assuming that you feel crappy likewise praise yourself for what you in all actuality do as opposed to zeroing in on what you didn't do. Assuming you just stroll for 10mins as opposed to whipping yourself for just doing 10mins, let yourself know it's fabulous that you followed through with something

This is the kind of thing I battle with constantly. I've understood: when you beat yourself up, you are additionally thrashing everybody around you this. It's depleting for them. You do it so somebody will step in and let you know that "it's alright" and "you're fine and we love you!" But that main works for such a long time. However, it's simply moment delight. Unadulterated masturbation.

Understand that you are a strong individual, and by whipping yourself, you're utilizing that ability to cause others to feel as sorry for you as you accomplish for yourself. Ponder what it resembles for them to continually watch somebody they love hit themselves upside the head. It's depleting.

Rather than attempting to change yourself and your propensities and your life and all that you disdain about yourself, begin by just tolerating yourself for what your identity is. Part of being positive and propelled and cherishing yourself is seeing the individual you're putting out into the world. Escape your head and onto the court.

"However, I can't! Its excessively! Im not sufficient!" You'll say. Well stop it. That is simply seriously thrashing yourself.

Need to know how to escape your head? Need to know how to quit considering yourself to be terrible or languid or idiotic? Go work on something for another person. Go be liberal. Go worker. Go tell somebody something great. Learn something. Enhance the world. Grin. Relax. You are awesome, entire and complete similarly as you are. Acknowledge your defects and utilize your ability to accomplish something caring. Really buckle down. Pardon yourself. Quit searching for a response and simply acknowledge each second as it works out. Be generous and kind.

at the point when you take a walk pay attention to great web recordings/YouTube videos and so forth on confidence, cherishing yourself, joy, objective setting, profound cleanliness and so on be kind with yourself and recall when u gander at others do u see their blemishes and lines and flaws or do you simply see your companion, your mum, your coworker? Others don't see us like we see us so be kind with yourself

on the off chance that somebody addressed you the manner in which you address you could you keep them around? On the off chance that u called a companion and said I just had a downright terrible date with a fellow and they said "well no big surprise you're exhausting and fat, nobody could need you around" could you actually converse with that individual? You'd be like "wtf is off with you buddy? For what reason are u being so frightful, what's up with you?!" When that inward voice begins talking say hello (give it a name say Lisa) say hello Lisa, you're a bitch, shut your face, that is phony information! :P

one more enormous move forward for me was getting a cat having something to endlessly cherish me back was tremendous! Besides every one of the chuckles and tomfoolery

Try not to be challenging for yourself assuming you have absolutely crappy days that u spend in bed. It will pass. You might need to think about conversing with somebody for additional assistance

Chapter 4

Ways Getting Help

On the off chance that injury is behind your self-loathing, think about looking for proficient assistance. Whether a specialist, clergyman, or otherworldly instructor, proficient help can empower you to comprehend the foundation of your self-hatred and move toward self-empathy.

Bogus Expectations

It is typical to need to have a place, be acknowledged, or play out an undertaking great. Notwithstanding, once in a while our assumptions for self can be high to the point that they are unreachable by any human. These exceptional assumptions frequently lead to us missing the mark and feeling as though we have fizzled.

At these times, our internal pundit makes an appearance to disgrace us and remind us how disheartening we have been. Regardless of whether our reasonable side perceives that the assumptions are outlandish, our inward pundit keeps on driving home proclamations of self-loathing.

Endeavors to Please Others

With an end goal to be associated with others, we might have learned after some time that living up to the assumptions of others functions admirably. We could learn through friendly encounters that when others are content with us, we can feel content with ourselves. This undesirable perspective about connections might try and prompt critical examples of ward conduct.

Regardless, certain individuals feel crushed when they can't address the issues of others or they believe they have frustrated somebody. Proclamations of self-loathing recommend that when we don't measure up to the assumptions of others something is off with us; we have fizzled or we are not deserving of being cherished or esteemed by others.

Hairsplitting

A stickler is frequently seen as somebody who permits themselves no safety buffer, no space for error for human mix-ups or limits. They anticipate flawlessness of themselves (and conceivably others) consistently and in all circumstances.

It is essential to take note of that we frequently foster a stickler mentality with an end goal to safeguard ourselves from agony and sensations of disconnection.3 The conviction is that when you perform impeccably, you are some way or another keeping yourself from feeling torment. This aggravation might incorporate sensations of disgrace, shame, dejection, relinquishment, derision, judgment, and the sky is the limit from there.

Social Comparison

While it is typical to glance around and notice what others are doing, it can become agonizing when you put esteem on that perception. On the off chance that you experience self-loathing, it is normal to have what is alluded to as up correlation. This basically implies tending to just notification and give worth to individuals who are performing "better" and, thusly, cheapening yourself with articulations of self-loathing.

The Tolls of Self-Hatred

Self-loathing influences and impacts numerous parts of everyday living. Self-loathing can keep you from settling on significant choices, facing challenges, interfacing with others, and accomplishing objectives. Assuming you battle with self-loathing, you might encounter its ramifications in numerous areas and ways.

Relationship With Self

Of course, self-loathing as an adverse consequence on self-idea (the picture you have of yourself) as well as confidence (how you feel about yourself). At the point when your internal pundit is continually putting yourself down, seeing yourself in a positive light is almost unthinkable.

The Workplace

Since work is many times execution based (acting a specific way, meeting position assumptions, collaborating with others), it isn't is business as usual that self-loathing can influence your work life. At the point when you feel useless or unable, you might be less inclined to take on activities or find it challenging to work cooperatively with others. You might feel disdain toward associates or put yourself down for absence of execution.

Social Situations

It tends to be incredibly hard to make and keep up with companionships when you are troubled with consistent and constant negative self-talk and self-hatred. To stay away from the aggravation of analysis, judgment, or relinquishment, you might try and oppose meeting new individuals. Or then again you might put on a show of being cold or unfeeling, which can keep you from drawing near to other people.

Family Relationships

Since a critical effect on self-loathing comes from past friendly encounters like maltreatment and injury, relational intricacies can feel extremely confounded for somebody battling with self-loathing. You might be in a circumstance that expects you to be in touch with somebody from your difficult past, making trouble and a propensity pull out with an end goal to try not to encounter excruciating recollections and feelings.

Regardless of whether you are not managing a horrendous family ancestry, your fussbudget outlook and unreasonable assumptions for self can hinder having the option to appreciate family interactions.3 The strain to "performing impeccably" in those settings can turn out to be excessively and keep you from framing or potentially getting a charge out of family associations.

Close connections

Close connections can feel muddled and mistaking for somebody who encounters self-loathing. You might battle the possibility of closeness and closeness.

Regardless of whether you long to feel close, the anxiety toward somebody seeing your apparent flaws, impediments, or absence of significant worth can be overpowering and hold up traffic of a significant relationship.4 The inward pundit is sufficiently difficult, however the prospect of somebody near you seeing or figuring those things about you can feel obliterating.

Objective Setting

Self-loathing lets us know that we are not competent and will probably fizzle or miss the mark — and this kind of reasoning can make objectives, wants, and dreams feel far off and inconceivable. You might take a gander at others and think they are hitting the nail on the head, while you experience the ill effects of steady self-basic explanations. Living this way is genuinely debilitating and can bring about an absence of want to define objectives by any means.

Independent direction

Negative self-talk and self-hatred can seize or deaden thinking skills. At the point when you see yourself in such a negative manner, you might feel less able to face challenges that will assist you with developing. You might pull away from potential chances to interface with others and end up trapped in an example of self-question.

Chapter 5

Instructions to Stop the Cycle of Self-Loathing

Living with self-loathing is overpowering, debilitating, and disconnecting. Fortunately, there are steps we can take to calm that internal pundit, quiet the negative tempest, and push ahead in certain ways.

Tame Your Inner Critic

In the event that you battle with self-loathing, your internal pundit could feel persistent and you might start trusting your inward exchange's scornful account. At the point when this occurs, it is useful to attempt to dial yourself back and recognize sentiments from reality.

Stock Your Strengths

Distinguishing your assets can assist with calming self-loathing. In the event that you find it hard to concoct some all alone, think about asking others for help. It is quite often more straightforward to remember another person's assets as opposed to our own.

Figure out how to Accept Compliments

In the event that you view yourself in a contemptuous manner, taking a compliment is hard. It might try and feel unfamiliar and awkward thus you'll excuse it or limit to try not to feel helpless.

Figuring out how to acknowledge a commendation will take practice, yet it is conceivable. The following time somebody praises you, take a stab at saying "much obliged" — and stop there. Fight the temptation to follow it up with a self-basic or cavalier reaction

Foster Self-Compassion

Individuals who battle with self-loathing frequently have next to zero sympathy toward themselves. Truth be told, having self-sympathy can feel incomprehensible or confounding. An incredible method for considering self-empathy is to ponder the way that you would treat a companion or cherished one. Could you thrash them for committing an error or advise them that nobody is great?

Therapist and self-sympathy analyst Kristin Neff, PhD, makes sense of:

"Rather than hardheartedly judging and censuring yourself for different insufficiencies or deficiencies, self-empathy implies you are caring and understanding when stood up to with individual downfalls. All things considered, whoever said you should be great?"

Practice Forgiveness

Self-loathing is in many cases zeroed in on the past — an excruciating second or feeling like disgrace or responsibility, outrage or shame, or a feeling of weakness. There, there is no space to excuse ourselves or embrace what our identity is.

Give your all to remain in the present and spotlight on how far you have come. This might feel awkward or unique, however after some time, it will assist you with diminishing self-loathing and gain self-sympathy

A Word From authour

Recollect that halting self-loathing takes time. It could feel testing and incomprehensible on occasion. You might try and wind up lamenting this intimately acquainted piece of you, which is OK. At the point when you permit yourself to relinquish the negative pundit, you account for more satisfaction, harmony, and association in your life.

Chapter 6

Self-hatred Therapy

While you can work on self-hatred all alone, searching out proficient help is in every case best. Seeking treatment will permit you to investigate different adapting procedures to make your self-hatred designs disappear. However, there is more than one sort of treatment, and picking only one can challenge.

For instance, certain individuals advocate for care intercessions, which will help you to know about your sentiments from an external perspective. Through various strategies, the specialist will show you how to challenge your negative perspectives on yourself through contemplation.

Others rather suggest conventional treatment, as it can show you esteems like self-empathy and generosity. Furthermore, it will likewise help you to see the value in self-analysis when it's not over the top.

Working on Self-Loathing all alone

There are a few general ideas that can help anybody going through a period of self-hatred. Regardless of whether you go to treatment, these key rules can assist you with keeping focused — and stop the repetitive, self-loathing designs.

Attempt to notice your contemplations from an external perspective. As we've previously referenced, care activities can assist you with monitoring your contemplations in a nonjudgmental manner. This will permit you to perceive and defend self-hatred designs so you can stop them in time.

Impact the manner in which you converse with yourself. Frequently, we converse with ourselves in a negative way, pushing thoughts of not being sufficient or offending ourselves. All things considered, take a stab at envisioning you're addressing a close buddy that is going through exactly the same things as you.

Bring down your assumptions. A major part of self-hatred is that it makes you put forth ridiculous assumptions and objectives — normally because of unreasonable correlations with others. By setting sensible, effectively attainable objectives, you'll support your confidence and diminish disdain related contemplations.

Attempt to acknowledge being sufficient. Society frequently pushes us to accept that we ought to be awesome — however it's OK to be basic, furious, and wrong now and again. Rather than disdaining these feelings, attempt to embrace them and acknowledge that occasionally being sufficiently great is alright.

Offer something positive to yourself. An extraordinary approach to rapidly helping your confidence is offering something good to yourself consistently. For instance, praise yourself for doing the dishes, or congratulate yourself for finishing that monotonous schoolwork.

Indications of Self-Hatred

The following are a portion of the indications that you may be living with self-loathing, past having incidental negative self-talk.

Go big or go home reasoning:

You consider yourself and your life to be either fortunate or unfortunate, with no shades of in the middle between. In the event that you commit an error, you feel like everything is demolished or that you're a disappointment.

Center around the negative:

Regardless of whether you have a decent day, you will generally zero in on the terrible things that occurred or what turned out badly all things considered.

Profound thinking:

You accept your sentiments as realities. In the event that you notice that you are feeling terrible or like a disappointment, you expect that your sentiments should mirror the reality of the matter and that you are, truth be told, terrible.

Low confidence:

You by and large have low confidence and don't feel like you measure up while contrasting yourself with others in day to day existence.

Looking for endorsement:

You are continually looking for outside endorsement from others to approve your self-esteem. Your assessment of yourself changes relying upon how others assess you or their thought process of you.

Can't acknowledge praises:

Assuming somebody praises you, you rebate information exchanged or feel that they are simply being great. You experience difficulty tolerating praises and will generally dismiss them rather than thoughtfully tolerating them.

Attempting to fit in: You find that you generally feel like an outcast and are continuously attempting to find a place with others. You feel like individuals loathe you and can't comprehend the reason why they would need to invest energy with you or really like you.

Thinking about analysis literally: You struggle when somebody offers analysis, and will quite often accept it as an individual assault or consider it long sometime later.

Frequently feeling desirous: You find yourself envious of others and may chop them down to help yourself have an improved outlook on your circumstance throughout everyday life.

Unfortunate of positive associations: You might drive away companions or possible accomplices out of dread when somebody gets excessively close, and accept that it will end gravely or you will wind up alone.

Tossing pity parties for yourself: You tend to toss feel sorry for parties for you and feel like you have been managed a terrible parcel throughout everyday life, or that everything is stacked against you.

Reluctant to think beyond practical boundaries: You are hesitant to have dreams and goals and feel like you really want to keep on carrying on with your life in a safeguarded manner. You might fear disappointment, scared of progress, or peer down on yourself paying little heed to what you accomplish.

Hard on yourself: If you commit an error, you have an exceptionally difficult time excusing yourself. You may likewise have laments about things you have done previously or neglected to do. You might experience difficulty giving up and moving previous mishaps.

Critical perspective: You see the world in an exceptionally negative manner and disdain the world that you live in. You feel like individuals with an uplifting perspective are credulous about the way that the world truly works. You don't see things improving and have an extremely distressing point of view.

Chapter 7

Instructions to Combat Self-Hatred

In the event that you are hoping to move past self-loathing, there are various things you can do to break the cycle. Regardless of anything else, recall that you are not to fault for how you feel, but rather you are dependable from this day forward for the moves that you initiate toward rolling out good improvements.

Take a stab at Journaling

Keep a diary to consider your day and how you had an outlook on what occurred. Consider the occasions of the day, analyze circumstances that might have set off specific feelings, and be aware of the main drivers of any identity contempt.

As you diary every day, search for examples and plan to turn out to be more mindful of how your feelings shift. Research shows that expressive composing, for example, journaling can assist with lessening mental distress.5

Disrespect Your Inner Critic

As you begin to turn out to be more mindful of your feelings and their triggers, attempt to recognize the contemplations that you have when confronted with pessimistic occasions. Ask yourself inquiries about whether your contemplations are reasonable, or whether you are taking part in thought twists.

Have a go at facing your inward harasser by countering that internal voice with contentions going against the norm. In the event that you find it hard to develop areas of strength for an all alone, envision yourself assuming the job of a more grounded individual you know — like a companion, celebrity, or hero — and sassing the basic voice in your mind.

Practice Self-Compassion

Rather than abhorring yourself, work on showing yourself empathy. This implies taking a gander at circumstances from an alternate perspective, seeing the beneficial things that you have achieved, and finishing dark or-white reasoning. What might you tell a companion or cherished one who was having comparable considerations about themselves?

Was that something awful that happened actually the apocalypse? Could you reexamine what is happening to consider it to be a mishap rather than a calamity? At the point when you can be kinder to yourself, you'll free yourself up to additional good sentiments and a positive internal voice. Research shows that empathy centered treatment can work on confidence, which could be useful to decrease self-hatred.6

Invest Energy With Positive People

Rather than spending time with individuals who cause you to feel awful, begin spending time with individuals who encourage you. On the off chance that you have no certain individuals your day to day existence, consider joining a care group. In the event that you don't know where to find one, the National Alliance on Mental Illness is a decent spot to begin, paying little mind to what kind of emotional well-being issues you may confront.

Deal with Yourself

Rather than participating in pointless ways of behaving, take part in taking care of oneself. This approach implies dealing with your physical and psychological wellness by doing everything that will keep you feeling better. Eat good food, get ordinary activity, get sufficient rest, lessen web-based entertainment and screen time, invest energy in nature, and talk merciful to yourself, to give some examples models.

Push Toward Living the Life You Want

The remedy to feeling terrible all the time may be to begin moving toward what you need throughout everyday life. That could mean tracking down another profession way, voyaging, escaping obligation, cutting off a friendship, beginning a family, or moving far away. Decide your qualities and afterward begin acting as per them. When you begin to line up with your qualities, feeling sure about yourself will be simpler.

It's not difficult to believe that you are the one in particular who battles with contemplations of self-loathing. Truly many individuals feel the same way that you do, and there are ways of moving beyond it.

Assuming you're actually attempting to move past these sentiments, it may be the case that a hidden psychological wellness issue is adding to your negative reasoning examples. On the off chance that you haven't proactively been evaluated by an emotional well-being proficient, this ought to be your initial step. In the event that you are determined to have a psychological problem, this could be the beginning stage to at long last rolling out certain improvements in your day to day existence.

Then again, in the event that you don't have a diagnosable problem, or on the other hand assuming you have previously seen an emotional wellness proficient and are getting treatment, then, at that point, your best strategy is to finish your treatment plan and think about attempting a portion of the previously mentioned set of ways of dealing with hardship or stress to deal with your pessimistic reasoning.

In the event that this feels hard, you could profit from a responsibility accomplice or another person who will check in with you routinely to ensure that you are staying aware of your good propensities. While it could feel hard to trust in somebody that you want assistance, you additionally may be amazed at how willing others will be to help when you inquire.

There's no great explanation to continue to carry on with your existence with the considerations about abhorring yourself. Today, you can venture out toward feeling quite a bit improved and carrying on with a daily existence that isn't loaded up with self-loathing and pessimistic idea designs.

Ways Of closing the Door on Self-Hatred

1. Focus on your triggers

The initial step to resolving any issue is grasping its root.

In the event that you're engaging a serious episode of self-loathing, it tends to be useful to sit with that inclination and attempt to distinguish where it came from. You don't live in a vacuum, so consider what might have provoked these sentiments.

You've heard it multiple times, yet journaling can truly help here. Have a go at taking a seat by the day's end and stroll during your time intellectually. Attempt to write down certain notes about:

what you did

how you felt during various exercises

who you were with over the course of the day

In the event that you don't deal with best by composing, you can record brief recordings or voice notices for yourself on your telephone. You can likewise basically reflect for a couple of seconds on the occasions of the day.

Notwithstanding the way in which you approach unloading your day, attempt to look out for any ongoing ideas or examples that could end up being useful to you distinguish what sets off your negative contemplations.

Whenever you've recognized a portion of your triggers, you can deal with thinking of ways of keeping away from or limit them. There are a few triggers you probably won't have the option to keep away from, so it's useful to gain proficiency with the devices to manage them.

2. Challenge your negative contemplations

In some cases self-loathing springs up when you're not in a decent spot to diary or reflect. At the point when this occurs, take a stab at having an inside discussion with yourself.

For instance, on the off chance that you think, "I disdain myself," it tends to be useful to inquire, "Why?" If the response is, "I look appalling in this dress," or "I truly wrecked that gathering," then have a go at testing that idea too right away.

Tell yourself, "That is false." Then consider reasons this negative idea is off-base.

Confronting your own considerations can feel overwhelming. Assuming that is the situation, take a stab at envisioning a different distinguish to battle your contemplations. Perhaps they're a blend of all your most loved superheroes from youth or a dearest companion. Envision them coming in and shutting down those negative or testing those negative contemplations.

Cheer up in the event that the positive side of things doesn't win. Just testing these pessimistic considerations assists with building up the possibility that self-loathing isn't a reality or irrefutable truth — it's an inclination.

3. Practice positive self-talk

Self-loathing frequently arrives in a second when you don't have empathy for yourself. In the event that you have a period where you're feeling better, attempt to work out a rundown of what you love about yourself.

On the off chance that you can't imagine anything, don't overreact. Love is serious areas of strength for a that is difficult to feel toward yourself in a depressed spot. On the off chance that it's more straightforward, attempt to consider things you essentially like or don't can't stand about yourself.

Perhaps you take great consideration of your pet or consistently know exactly what to bring to a potluck.

Keep this rundown where you'll see it consistently. At the point when the self-loathing contemplations come, stop, calmly inhale, and say without holding back one of the things from your rundown.

4. Rethink your negative contemplations

Reexamining is a treatment method that can be utilized to address negative considerations and self-loathing. It's typically finished by basically moving your contemplations to a marginally alternate point of view.

It could include thinking potential gains about a terrible circumstance or taking into account a dissatisfaction in another light. Anyway you choose to attempt it, reevaluating is tied in with preparing your cerebrum to find and zero in on the positive.

For instance, rather than saying, "I'm so terrible working introductions," you could reevaluate the assertion to, "I don't feel as I did well in my show today."

Indeed, it's a little change. Yet, you're taking a go big or go home proclamation and reevaluating it as a solitary occurrence.

This helps the antagonism not feel so overpowering or extremely durable. All things considered, wrecking one work show is just a single example — and it implies you can improve sometime later.

The following time you want to say, "I disdain myself," attempt to consider a little way you can reexamine that assertion to be more sensible and explicit.

5. Invest energy with individuals who satisfy you

Self-loathing can make you need to disconnect. You could feel as you don't merit being around your companions or family. Or then again you could feel like nobody even needs to associate with you.

While pulling out from social circumstances might seem like the best activity as per our negative self-talk, studies have shown this isn't smart.

Interfacing with others is an immense piece of our psychological prosperity since social connection assists us with resting easier thinking about ourselves. It establishes a climate wherein we feel esteemed and really focused on.

The most effective way to battle these negative contemplations is to invest energy with our friends and family, whether that is a companion, relative, or accomplice. Go for an espresso, see a film together, or basically visit while going for a stroll together. Social collaboration can assist you with feeling re-energized and esteemed.

6. Practice self-empathy

This might be the hardest thing on the rundown, yet all the same it's maybe the most accommodating.

Self-empathy is not quite the same as self esteem. It implies tolerating your negative contemplations, missteps, and disappointments, and figuring out them as chaotic human minutes.

It implies pardoning yourself similarly you'd excuse a friend or family member for raging at you in a snapshot of disappointment.

The following time you end up spiraling down the self-loathing deep, dark hole, attempt to give yourself a little room to breath. Recognize that you're not feeling perfect and advise yourself that is totally fine.

Harping on specific activities you've taken that you're not pleased with? Advise yourself that no one's perfect. Those activities don't need to characterize you.

Obviously, self-empathy doesn't work out pretty much by accident. Yet, studies have shown that, similar as reexamining or contemplation, self-sympathy is a teachable expertise.

7. Request help

Keep in mind: You're never alone in your psychological well-being venture. Everybody has been where you are at some point, and most need a little assistance to overcome.

It's smart to rehearse the things on this rundown with the assistance of a confided in psychological wellness proficient. There's no disgrace in requesting help. As a matter of fact, it's the most effective way to figure out how to deal with your self-loathing and negative self-talk.

The specialty of self esteem and self acknowledgment.

Self esteem is sympathy and unrestricted acknowledgment for yourself. It's dealing with and addressing your own requirements and permitting non-judgemental thinking. It is seeing yourself as basically commendable, great, significant, and meriting bliss.

At the point when you love yourself, you will feel less anxious or awkward while going through troublesome occasions or circumstances. You will not contend with or contrast yourself with others. You'll embrace your difficulties. You'll turn into a hopeful mastermind, and you'll get imaginative and attempt new things

Ways Self Love Will Change Your Life

1. Wellbeing

At the point when you love yourself, you'll deal with your body and prosperity. You'll eat better. You'll move your body, keeping in mind your body. Since your body strives to keep you alive and allowing you to carry on with your life, you deal with it consequently. You focus on taking care of oneself on the grounds that your psychological prosperity is similarly all around as significant as your actual prosperity.

2. Connections

We acknowledge the adoration we assume we merit. At the point when you genuinely love yourself, you set the norm to acknowledge excellent love consequently. You have low capacity to bear individuals who don't esteem you or regard you. At the point when you regard yourself, others will regard you as well.

3. Certainty

Self esteem additionally supports your certainty. Since you love and embrace all that you will be, you're not shaky or embarrassed about it. You display what you got. You feel lovely, you feel strong. You hold your head as high as possible and have a great time throughout everyday life.

4. Style and Swag

Alongside certainty comes your extraordinary style and loot. At the point when your confidence is high, you have a particular style that you remarkably you. You've developed to know yourself, your preferences and your stylish. Essentially, you understand what you like and you won't hesitate to show it. This shows itself in your special eye sore.

5. Companions and Family

Confidence will likewise change your associations with your companions and family. Rather than saying "OK" to others' solicitations, you will actually want to express no to things that don't serve you, since you esteem and safeguard your own energy. You love yourself an excessive amount to allow yourself to endure to the detriment of others. Having self esteem will likewise make it more straightforward for you to excuse other people who have harmed you. You understand that it just damages you to hold a negative resentment inside, so in light of the fact that you love and care about yourself, you figure out how to give up and excuse.

6. Joy

This one's a given however worth focusing on: Self love will make you more joyful. When you love somebody, you maintain that they should be blissful, correct? So when you love yourself, you will give your best for satisfy YOU. It's astonishing. By cherishing the skin you're in and the spirit that you will be, you offer yourself the chance to carry on with your best life.

7. Drive and Motivation

You'll likewise be more determined and roused throughout everyday life. Since you have high self-esteem, you know your limitless potential to make esteem on the planet. You realize you can achieve anything assuming that you put your energy into it. You don't agree to any less, on the grounds that you realize you are able to do quite a lot more.

8. Less F*cks Given

A significant advantage of confidence is that you'll mind such a lot of less about others' thought process of you and what others say regarding you. Inspirational tones just ✋ You figure out how to keep just individuals who really love and care about you in your inward circle. Anything beyond that doesn't make any difference.

9. Simpler Failures (Positive Self Talk)

Assuming that you at any point come up short or screw up, rather than being no picnic for yourself, you are kinder to yourself and faster to excuse. That is the sorcery of adoration: all is generally great. Contemplate how you would converse with a friend or family member, or a blameless kid or pet. You would treat them with adoration. On the off chance that they mess up, it's OK. Attempt once more tomorrow. Rather than pummeling yourself over your mix-ups, you'll be kinder and more wanting to yourself.

10. Less Insecurities, More Humility

At the point when you really love yourself, you won't have to feel shaky and contrast yourself with others. Since you can cherish yourself, you can transparently adore others as well. You can be steady rather than desirous or jealous. Life doesn't need to feel like a rivalry since you comprehend that everybody is exceptional and brings extraordinary worth that can't be recreated. You remain steadfast in what your identity is and you support people around you, lifting them up. You are modest on the grounds that you don't have to *act* like you're really great.

11. Opportunity

Above all, confidence will liberate you. Consider it. What can keep you down when you are your own closest companion, truly adoring and supporting yourself all through this whole excursion of life? Nothing and nobody can keep you down. You are allowed to step into your significance. You are allowed to be impressive. You are allowed to be a light on the planet. You are allowed to act naturally.

Step by step instructions to Turn Self-Hatred into Self-Compassion

Converse with yourself the manner in which you converse with somebody you care about:

In Compassion and Self Hate, Dr. Rubin encourages perusers to tell themselves, "I treat myself as I treat a kid I love." Cognitive social specialists utilize a comparative method, frequently conjuring the inquiry, "What might you share with an old buddy who was going through exactly the same thing you are going through?" These are significant inquiries. Assuming you disdain yourself, you probably express things to yourself that you wouldn't think for even a second to share with someone else. What might you tell another person who has precisely the same characteristics as you? What might you at any point tell yourself?

Perceive that convictions don't approach bits of insight: Often, individuals accept everything they say to themselves. On the off chance that you assume you are a failure, you might accept it is unadulterated fact of the matter. Attempt this mental social method called "the three C's": get, check, change. Discover yourself thinking something negative about yourself. Check whether your troubling idea is valid. Transform it, if not. You can disrespect your negative considerations.

Challenge them. Act as a guard lawyer to the examiner in your mind.

Understand that suppositions don't necessarily compare to realities: People often accept everything they say to themselves. You could think it is irrefutably valid on the off chance that you accept you are a failure. Attempt this "three C's" mental social procedure: get, check, change. Become mindful of any decisive contemplations you have about yourself. Confirm the veracity of your disturbing supposition. In the event that not, alter it. Your negative considerations can be countered. Go up against them. Shield yourself against the arraignment in your viewpoints.

Embrace the idea of "adequate":

Many individuals feel they ought to be awesome — never irate, consistently liberal, never basic, in every case right, etc. These assumptions reject that blemish is the human condition. In the event that you are one of these individuals with too-elevated standards for yourself, ask your self what is Self-Loathing

Think about going to otherworldliness or religion:

Numerous profound or strict customs community on the conviction that individuals are imperfect however innately great, adorable as well as intrinsically cherished. These convictions can act as a tremendous demulcent for the stinging soul. The acts of reflection and care, as well, can cultivate identity sympathy as well as cherishing benevolence toward others.

If you hate yourself for mistakes you made, make amends:

You might be understanding this and thinking, "This doesn't concern me. I accomplished something so horrendous that I can never be excused." First, however much you denounce yourself, inquire as to whether you would similarly sentence — to their face — another person who did likewise. In the event that not, then, at that point, you are being uncalled for to yourself. Maybe you truly accomplished something dreadful. In the event that you can't offer to set things right to the individual or individuals you hurt, help another person. Whipping on yourself serves no one. Accomplishing something useful for other people or partaking in a bigger development not just helps other people, it helps you — and it can prompt self-pardoning.

Attempt treatment:

A decent, humane specialist can assist you with encouraging self-sympathy and better grasp the foundations of your self-hatred.

ways of practicing confidence

In a general sense, confidence is for the most part about dealing with our inward pundit so we can foster a more nuanced perspective on our disappointments, and value all our work and self-awareness in a sort, cherishing, and conscious way towards ourselves.

Keep away from negative self-talk.

In her book, Dr. Kristin Neff inquires: "What kind of language do you use with yourself when you notice a blemish or commit an error? Do you affront yourself or do you take a more kind and figuring out tone? Assuming you are profoundly self-basic, how does that cause you to feel inside?" Paying thoughtfulness regarding how you inside converse with yourself is the main move toward figuring out how to develop confidence.

Make individual ceremonies.

The principal contrast among propensities and customs is the manner by which mindful and deliberate you are. Customs are significant practices with a profound feeling of direction. Remove time from your bustling day for taking care of oneself customs, whether it's giving adoration to your body by working out, or giving affection to your psyche by thinking.

Put down sound stopping points.

It tends to be difficult to adore yourself when individuals around you are not regarding your time or recognizing your worth, whether at work or in your everyday existence. Escaping the yes autopilot and figuring out how to express no to safeguard your significant investment is a strong method for rehearsing self esteem.

Be sympathetic towards yourself.

Self-sympathy is basically the same as being empathetic towards others. It comprises in seeing that you are enduring and offering yourself getting it and benevolence. As Dr. Kristin Neff puts it: " You might attempt to change in manners that permit you to be more solid and blissful, however this is done on the grounds that you care about yourself, not on the grounds that you are useless or unsuitable as you are."

Account for self-reflection.

Some of the time, things don't go to design. Rather than accusing yourself, bomb like a researcher so you can gain from these disappointments and use them as a chance for self-awareness. Self-reflection can appear as a journaling practice, a week by week survey, or a normal gathering with a confided in companion to ponder your new encounters and difficulties.

As may be obvious, only a couple of changes can sustain more confidence. These progressions can be pretty much as basic as valuing our persistent effort and endeavors without being excessively or brutally basic, taking on solid customs, and defining sound limits.

Confidence can prompt better psychological wellness, higher confidence, more inspiration, and numerous other proof based benefits. It needn't bother with to be messy. Check it out, and remember about the force of self-reflection. Disappointment isn't the apocalypse, it's a chance for learning and self-awareness

Self esteem movements to transform your life

Pay attention to your heart/internal voice.Discover and support your own gifts, assets, and abilities.

Be delicate on yourself/Learn not to be so unforgiving with yourself.

Find self-esteem from the inside, as opposed to from outside approval.

Change how you oversee and deal with your feelings.

Have appreciation.

Decide to see what you have, rather than what you need.

Know that what you find in others, you additionally find in yourself.

Practice appreciation towards all pieces of your body.

Confidence movements to completely change you

Pay attention to your heart/internal voice.Discover and sustain your own gifts, assets, and abilities.

Be delicate on yourself/Learn not to be so severe with yourself.

Find self-esteem from the inside, instead of from outer approval.

Change how you oversee and deal with your feelings.

Have appreciation.

Decide to see what you have, rather than what you need.

Know that what you find in others, you additionally find in yourself.

Practice appreciation towards all pieces of your body.

Conclusion

You are a unique and remarkable individual. Anything you set your mind to, you can achieve. Nothing in the world can prevent you from accomplishing your goals as long as you fully accept and love yourself.

www.ingramcontent.com/pod-product-compliance
Lightning Source LLC
LaVergne TN
LVHW012114160826
845678LV00014B/3099

9798355409456